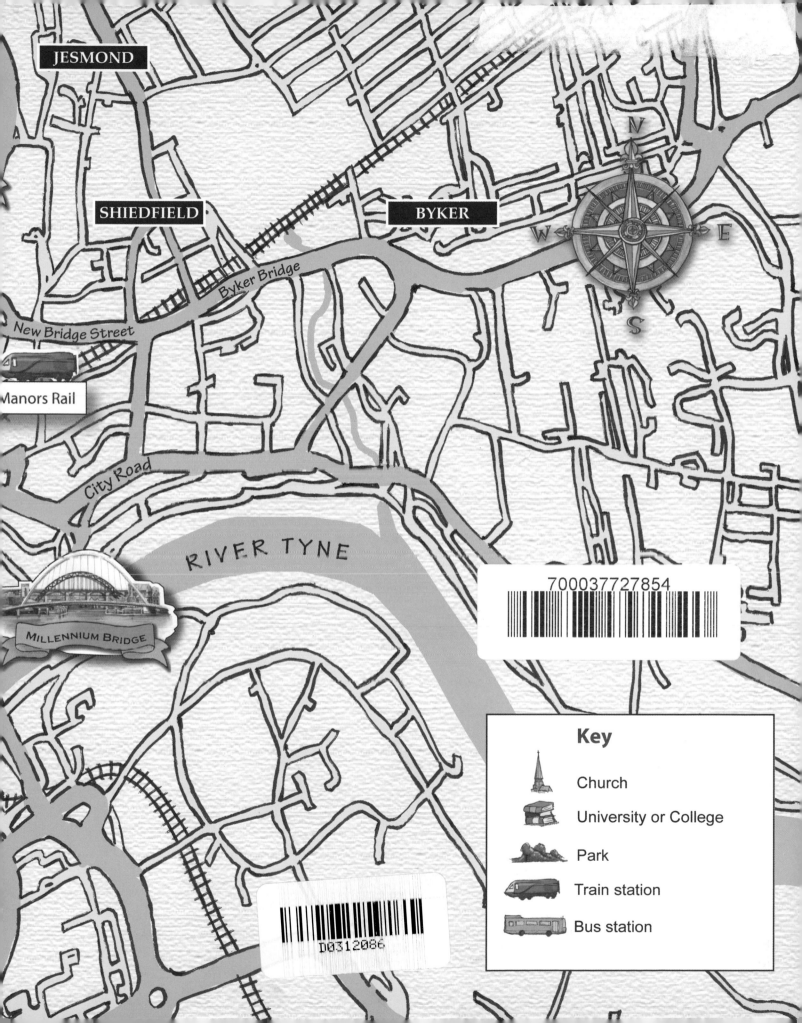

JESMOND

SHIEDFIELD

BYKER

Byker Bridge

New Bridge Street

Manors Rail

City Road

RIVER TYNE

MILLENNIUM BRIDGE

Key

Church

University or College

Park

Train station

Bus station

children's HISTORY of NEWCASTLE UPON TYNE

Written by
Peter Hepplewhite

HOMETOWN WORLD

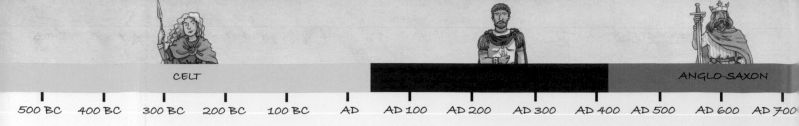

How well do you know your town?

Have you ever wondered what it would have been like living in Newcastle when the Romans arrived? What about fighting off invaders from Black Gate? This book will uncover the important and exciting things that happened in your town.

Want to hear the other good bits? You will love this book! Some rather brainy folk have worked on it to make sure it's fun and informative. So what are you waiting for? Peel back the pages and be amazed at what happened in your town.

THE FACTS

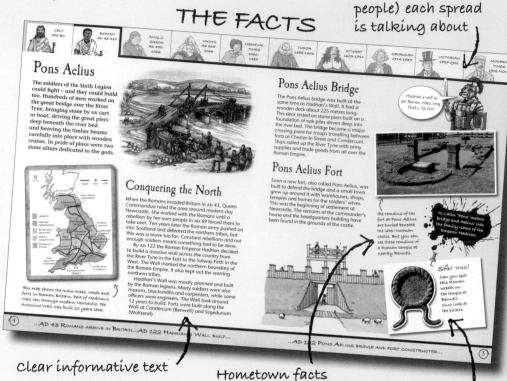

Timeline shows which period (dates and people) each spread is talking about

Clear informative text

Hometown facts to amaze you!

'Spot this!' game with hints on something to find in your town

THE EVIDENCE

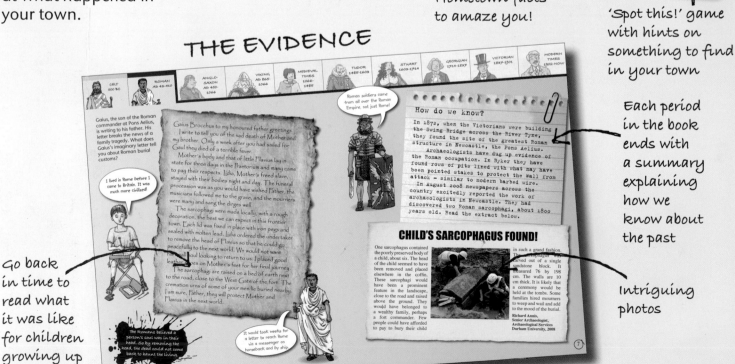

Go back in time to read what it was like for children growing up in Newcastle

Each period in the book ends with a summary explaining how we know about the past

Intriguing photos

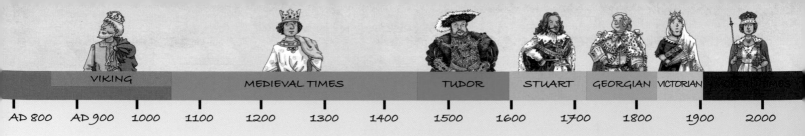

VIKING

MEDIEVAL TIMES

TUDOR

STUART

GEORGIAN

VICTORIAN

MODERN TIMES

AD 800   AD 900   1000   1100   1200   1300   1400   1500   1600   1700   1800   1900   2000

Contents

CELT
500 BC

ROMAN
AD 43-410

ANGLO-SAXON
AD 450-1066

VIKING
AD 865-1066

MEDIEVAL TIMES
1066-1485

Pons Aelius

The soldiers of the Sixth Legion could fight – and they could build too. Hundreds of men worked on the great bridge over the River Tyne, bringing stone by ox cart or boat, driving the great piers deep beneath the river bed and heaving the timber beams carefully into place with wooden cranes. In pride of place were two stone altars dedicated to the gods.

This map shows the main areas, roads and forts in Roman Britain. Part of Hadrian's Wall ran through modern Newcastle. The Antonine Wall was built 20 years later.

Conquering the North

When the Romans invaded Britain in AD 43, Queen Cartimandua ruled the area around modern-day Newcastle. She worked with the Romans until a rebellion by her own people in AD 69 forced them to take over. Ten years later the Roman army pushed on into Scotland and defeated the northern tribes, but this was a move too far. Constant rebellions and not enough soldiers meant something had to be done.

By AD 122 the Roman Emperor Hadrian decided to build a massive wall across the country from the River Tyne in the East to the Solway Firth in the West. The Wall marked the northern boundary of the Roman Empire. It also kept out the warring northern tribes.

Hadrian's Wall was mostly planned and built by the Roman legions. Many soldiers were also masons, blacksmiths and carpenters, while some officers were engineers. The Wall took around 12 years to build. Forts were built along the Wall at Condercum (Benwell) and Segedunum (Wallsend).

TUDOR
1485-1603

STUART
1603-1714

GEORGIAN
1714-1837

VICTORIAN
1837-1901

MODERN TIMES
1902-NOW

Pons Aelius Bridge

The Pons Aelius bridge was built at the same time as Hadrian's Wall. It had a wooden deck about 225 metres long. This deck rested on stone piers built on a foundation of oak piles driven deep into the river bed. The bridge became a major crossing point for troops travelling between forts at Chester-le-Street and Condercum. Ships sailed up the River Tyne with army supplies and trade goods from all over the Roman Empire.

Pons Aelius Fort

Soon a new fort, also called Pons Aelius, was built to defend the bridge and a small town grew up around it with warehouses, shops, temples and homes for the soldiers' wives. This was the beginning of settlement at Newcastle. The remains of the commander's house and the headquarters building have been found in the grounds of the castle.

Hadrian's wall is 80 Roman miles long. That's 118 km!

The remains of the fort at Pons Aelius are buried beneath the later Norman castle. But you can see these remains of a Roman temple at nearby Benwell.

In Latin 'Pons' means bridge and 'Aelius' was the family name of the Emperor Hadrian.

SPOT THIS!

Can you spot this Roman wreath on the temple at Benwell. Clue: look at the pillars.

CELT
500 BC

ROMAN
AD 43-410

ANGLO-SAXON
AD 450-1066

VIKING
AD 865-1066

MEDIEVAL TIMES
1066-1485

Gaius, the son of the Roman commander at Pons Aelius, is writing to his father. His letter breaks the news of a family tragedy. What does Gaius's imaginary letter tell you about Roman burial customs?

I lived in Rome before I came to Britain. It was much more civilized!

Gaius Brocchus to my honoured father, greetings. I write to tell you of the sad death of Mother and my brother. Only a week after you had sailed for Gaul they died of a terrible fever.

Mother's body and that of little Flavius lay in state for three days in the Praetorium and many came to pay their respects. Lidia, Mother's freed slave, stayed with their bodies night and day. The funeral procession was as you would have wished Father, the musicians followed me to the grave, and the mourners were many and sang the dirges well.

The sarcophagi were made locally, with a rough decoration, the best we can expect in this frontier town. Each lid was fixed in place with iron pegs and sealed with molten lead. Lidia ordered the undertaker to remove the head of Flavius so that he could go peacefully to the next world. We would not want his small soul looking to return to us. I placed good leather shoes on Mother's feet for her final journey.

The sarcophagi are raised on a bed of earth next to the road, close to the West Gate of the fort. The cremation urns of some of your men lie buried nearby. I am sure, Father, they will protect Mother and Flavius in the next world.

The Romans believed a person's soul was in their head. So by removing the head, the dead could not come back to haunt the living.

It took weeks for a letter to reach Rome via a messenger on horseback and by ship.

TUDOR
1485-1603

STUART
1603-1714

GEORGIAN
1714-1837

VICTORIAN
1837-1901

MODERN
TIMES
1902-NOW

Roman soldiers came from all over the Roman Empire, not just Rome!

How do we know?

In 1872, when the Victorians were building the Swing Bridge across the River Tyne, they found the site of the greatest Roman structure in Newcastle, the Pons Aelius. Archaeologists have dug up evidence of the Roman occupation. In Byker they have found rows of pits lined with what may have been pointed stakes to protect the Wall from attack – similar to modern barbed wire. In August 2008 newspapers across the country excitedly reported the work of archaeologists in Newcastle. They had discovered two Roman sarcophagi, about 1800 years old. Read the extract below.

CHILD'S SARCOPHAGUS FOUND!

One sarcophagus contained the poorly preserved body of a child, about six. The head of the child seemed to have been removed and placed elsewhere in the coffin. These sarcophagi would have been a prominent feature in the landscape, close to the road and raised above the ground. They would have belonged to a wealthy family, perhaps a fort commander. Few people could have afforded to pay to bury their child

in such a grand fashion. The sarcophagus was carved out of a single sandstone block. It measured 76 by 198 cm. The walls are 10 cm thick. It is likely that a ceremony would be held at the tombs. Some families hired mourners to weep and wail and add to the mood of the burial.

**Richard Annis,
Senior Archaeologist,
Archaeological Services
Durham University, 2008**

CELT
500 BC

ROMAN
AD 43-410

ANGLO-
SAXON
AD 450-
1066

VIKING
AD 865-
1066

MEDIEVAL
TIMES
1066-
1485

Invasion!

Ochta the monk sat at his desk and smoothed the parchment in front of him. He thought of the tales he had heard and began to picture what it must have been like watching the first Saxon ships sail up the River Tyne. The Romans had once ruled the Britons, he thought, but the Lord had chosen the Saxons to take over from them. Ochta dipped his quill pen in the ink pot and began to write.

Ad Murum

After the Roman army left Newcastle, around AD 410, some soldiers and their families stayed on Hadrian's Wall, living in the forts and farming the lands around. But they were no longer a powerful army. Without Roman protection, the British struggled to fight off invading tribes, like the Picts from Scotland. In desperation they hired Anglo-Saxon warriors from Denmark and Germany to help them fight.

The Anglo-Saxons drove away the invaders but then decided to stay. Under the Anglo-Saxons, Angle-Land, or England, become a patchwork of kingdoms, often at war with each another. For much of the 7th and 8th centuries Northumbria was one of the most powerful. At this time, Newcastle was a small manor known as Ad Murum, meaning 'next to the Wall'.

Map of Angle-Land

PICTLAND

Ad Murum
(Newcastle)

STRATHCLYDE

Hadrian's
Wall

N

NORTHUMBRIA

LINDSEY

EAST
ANGLIA

MERCIA

ESSEX

HWICCA

KENT

WESSEX   SUSSEX

The map shows the Anglo-Saxon kingdoms AD 600-900.

TUDOR
1485-1603

STUART
1603-1714

GEORGIAN
1714-1837

VICTORIAN
1837-1901

MODERN
TIMES
1902-NOW

Monkchester

There was another, more peaceful invasion going on. The pagan Angles were being converted to Christianity. On 11th April AD 627, King Edwin was baptized at York becoming the first Christian king of Northumbria. Around AD 674, Benedict Biscop founded the twin monasteries of St Peter's in Wearmouth and St Paul's in Jarrow. A small monastery was built near the old Roman fort at Newcastle. This became known as Monkchester. It was a golden age in Northumbria's past.

Monks, called scribes, kept hand-written records of events. Some of these scrolls and books survive today.

Vikings

But peace never lasted long in Anglo-Saxon Newcastle. In AD 793, monks at Lindisfarne recorded the first Viking raid on England. In AD 866 the Vikings came to settle at York. At first they ignored the area round the River Tyne but in AD 875 attacked Tynemouth and set up a base there. Northumbrian power was broken and the Vikings ruled in the North East.

Vikings Rule OK?

How do we know?

A monk known as the Venerable Bede (AD 673-735) lived at the monastery of St Paul's in nearby Jarrow. He was a great scholar. His most famous book is a History of the English People written about AD 731. It records in detail the history of Northumbria.

SPOT THIS!

An experiment to see if people from Newcastle could trace Viking ancestry through their DNA took place in this centre. Can you spot it?

CELT
500 BC

ROMAN
AD 43-410

ANGLO-
SAXON
AD 450-
1066

VIKING
AD 865-
1066

MEDIEVAL
TIMES
1066-1485

Border Wars

It is late in the summer of 1305 and an excited crowd has gathered round the Castle. The upper right quarter of the headless body of the Scottish hero, William Wallace, hangs from the Keep. His grisly remains have been sent from London where Wallace was executed as a traitor and his body hanged, drawn and quartered. He may be a hero in Scotland, but the people of Newcastle remember the blood-stained streets after his march through Northumberland in 1298.

The Newe Castle

William Wallace was one of many Scots who invaded Northumberland when England and Scotland were separate countries. Soon after the Normans conquered England in 1066, King William sent his eldest son, Robert Curthose, to the north. His task was to secure the bridge over the River Tyne against the Scots. Robert built a new wooden castle where the old Roman fort had stood. A small town sprang up around it and became known as 'Newe Castle'.

Robert's castle lasted about 100 years, but it wasn't strong enough to save the city. In 1138, Northumberland was invaded by King David of Scotland and the border with England moved south to the River Tees.

In 1174, William the Lion, King of Scotland, invaded Northumberland and was captured near Alnwick. He was held prisoner in Newcastle and later signed a peace treaty swearing loyalty to Henry II. A century later, William Wallace defeated a huge English army at the battle of Stirling Bridge. He followed this up by raiding and burning Hexham, Corbridge and Ryton.

King Henry II built the stone keep between 1172 and 1177. It was the strongest part of the Castle defences.

...1080 NEW WOODEN CASTLE BUILT...1172 CASTLE REBUILT IN STONE...

TUDOR
1485-1603

STUART
1603-1714

GEORGIAN
1714-1837

VICTORIAN
1837-1901

MODERN TIMES
1902-NOW

Walled City

In 1248 much of Newcastle, including the bridge, burnt down. From 1265, Newcastle citizens had to pay a tax for the construction of the city walls. They took around 50 years to build, but once completed merchants felt safe to trade and the city began to prosper. A new bridge was built too.

By 1372 the population had grown to around 4,000. Many people made a living farming, driving their cattle through the gates every morning onto common pasture on the Town Moor, Castle Leazes and Nun's Moor. On the east side of the city was Pandon, the industrial area where the stink of leather-making polluted the air.

We've got shops, houses and even a prison on our bridge!

The new stone bridge linked Newcastle with the little town of Gateshead.

William Wallace's other parts were sent to Berwick-upon-Tweed, Stirling and Aberdeen.

Quayside

The Quayside was Newcastle's port and trading centre. Wool, cloth, leather and fish were shipped from the Quayside out to sea. When border wars and cattle plagues devastated the countryside the coal trade took over. Coal mines opened at Elswick and on the Town Moor. Newcastle shipped tons of coal far and wide.

The movie 'Braveheart', starring Mel Gibson, tells the story of William Wallace

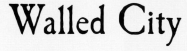

SPOT THIS!

Blackgate, built around 1247, was a gate house with a drawbridge at the front and another at the back. A portcullis was dropped down to seal the gate. Can you see the grooves it trundled down?

Guilds

Most skilled workers joined guilds. The most powerful guilds were groups of merchants who controlled trade, setting local prices and standards. Next came guilds of craftworkers like the tailors and tanners. They made rules about the working hours and conditions of their members. Each guild had a patron saint, celebrated festivals together and put on religious plays. They also looked after the health and wellbeing of their members and families.

CELT
500 BC

ROMAN
AD 43-410

ANGLO-
SAXON
AD 450-
1066

VIKING
AD 865-
1066

MEDIEVAL
TIMES
1066-1485

Bartolomeus, a novice monk at Blackfriars, is writing an entry in the monastery chronicle. This fictional account is based on real entries in local documents. What does he tell you about the effects of the long Scottish wars on Newcastle? Why are the people so hungry?

After all these years of training, I'm finally allowed to do some writing!

In the ninth year of the reign of King Edward (1316)

The Lord has turned his face away from Newcastle because of our sins. It is two grim years since that evil day when the Scottish King, Robert de Brus, destroyed the armies of our King at Bannockburn. Edward and others, to their everlasting shame, fled like miserable wretches to Dunbar Castle and took ship for Berwick, leaving the rest to their fate. Four thousand good men from Durham and Northumberland went to that desolate field and few came home. The name Bannockburn catches in English throats.

Now the Scots invade with cavalry and a large army. They have devastated almost all Northumberland with fire, except the castles. The people hide in the woods and there is terrible pestilence and death. Some poor folk are eating hounds, cats and horses because there are no oxen, kine (cattle) or sheep. Some, it is said, are so desperate they are eating the flesh of their own children.

Newcastle keep has three floors. This is a plan of the ground floor.

Chapel

Garrison Room

Ante-chamber

Mezzanine Chamber

Well

Plan of Newcastle Keep

TUDOR
1485-1603

STUART
1603-1714

GEORGIAN
1714-1837

VICTORIAN
1837-1901

MODERN
TIMES
1902-
NOW

The city wall was 3 km long, 2–3 m thick and up to 6 m high. With its six gates and 17 D-shaped towers the wall protected the city.

Robert Curthose built the 'Newe Castle' which gave Newcastle its name.

There were five small monasteries in Newcastle including Blackfriars, above, and Greyfriars.

How do we know?

We know that part of the body of William Wallace was sent to Newcastle because it was recorded in chronicles kept by monks like Bartolomeus. Monks living in monasteries wrote down the news as they heard it from eyewitnesses or rumours. William Wallace was captured and executed in 1305 on the orders of King Edward I. But a new, more dangerous Scottish king took over, Robert the Bruce. Robert defeated the English at Bannockburn in 1314. Chronicles from Newcastle have not survived, but the monastery at Lanercost recorded stirring tales of the border wars. Here are two extracts recorded from an eyewitness account:

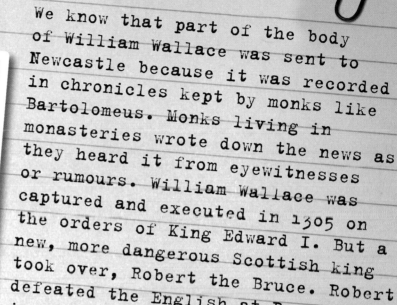

The Lanercost Chronicle

Before the battle they had to cross a great ditch into which the tide comes from the sea, called the Bannockburn...

...When in their confusion they tried to retreat, a great gorge engulfed many, and a great number died in it, while others avoided it with great difficulty.

Hazards and Riches

Mothers fearfully check their children for black blotches on their skin – or worse, pus-filled boils under their arms. Many families are packing their belongings and fleeing the city to live in the countryside until the curse has passed. The old and poor folk are staying in the town, praying that God will spare them and wearing masks to stifle the smell from the stinking streets. The plague is back in Newcastle again.

Crowded City

The weak and the sick were the first victims of two deadly diseases, the plague and sweating sickness. The crowded, narrow streets of Newcastle had open sewers and piles of reeking rubbish. This made a perfect breeding-ground for epidemics. By 1550 the population of Newcastle had grown to around 10,000, making it one of the largest cities in the country. In 1579, 2,000 people died of the plague. It returned 10 years later killing another 1,700 people.

During both outbreaks many frightened people left their homes and moved into camps outside the city walls But life was often hard and very short, with many children dying young. In winter families lived on preserved food. A pig or an ox from the Flesh Market would be slaughtered and the meat salted to last them until spring. With a shortage of fresh vegetables through the winter many people went hungry or were poorly nourished.

In 1539, Henry VIII closed down all the monasteries.

John Speed's map shows the city walls, streets and churches in 1610. Can you spot the bridge linking Newcastle and Gateshead?

...1513 BATTLE OF FLODDEN...1579 DEADLY PLAGUE HITS NEWCASTLE...

Border City

Living near the Scottish border added to the hazard of living in Newcastle. In 1513, King James IV of Scotland invaded England with an army of 35,000. The English army gathered at Newcastle before marching to Flodden Field. The English won a great victory, killing James and over half the Scottish nobles with him. Even so Newcastle had to be ready for further attacks. The townspeople paid taxes for the upkeep of the walls and had to be ready to defend them in times of danger. The muster rolls for 1539 list 1,097 able-bodied men who could become part-time soldiers.

Bessie Surtees House was built for merchants on Quayside in the 1600s. Bessie lived there with her father in the 1700s.

A Promise of Peace

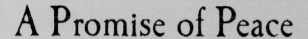

When Queen Elizabeth I died in 1603, King James VI of Scotland became James I of England. This seemed to promise peace for Newcastle. The new king stopped in Newcastle on his way to London to be crowned and was welcomed by happy crowds. He united the two countries and brought law and order to the borders. Hundreds of Border Reivers – gangs of cattle thieves and robbers – were executed or sent abroad.

Have you heard? Bessie Surtees eloped with John Scott! They ran away to Scotland to get married because her father didn't approve.

Coals from Newcastle

The new peace helped Newcastle to become one of the wealthiest towns in Britain. In 1600, Queen Elizabeth I had granted a powerful guild of merchants, known as the Hostmen, a charter giving them control of the local coal trade. In return they had to pay a tax of one-shilling for every wagonload of coal they exported. Newcastle was described as 'the Black Indies,' meaning coal was as profitable as the sugar and slave trades were for other cities.

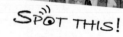

SPOT THIS!

City of Newcastle upon Tyne
THE GUILDHALL
Present building incorporates part of Robert Trollope's town court of 1655-8. North front (1796) by William Newton and David Stephenson; south front (1809); east end (1823) by John Dobson; altered 1880. Centre of town government until 1858.

Can you spot this blue plaque on the old Guildhall? There has been a guildhall building standing on this spot since 1400.

CELT
500 BC

ROMAN
AD 43-410

ANGLO-
SAXON
AD 450-
1066

VIKING
AD 865-
1066

MEDIEVAL
TIMES
1066-
1485

William Allen, a 14-year-old apprentice, is writing his journal in 1554. This imaginary journal is based on real decisions made by the Guild of Merchant Adventurers that cold winter. What does William tell you about how young people were behaving in the 1550s in Newcastle?

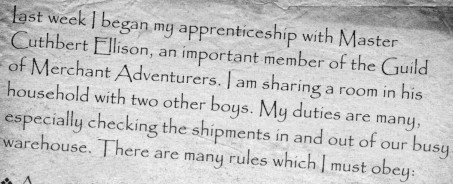

It's not much fun being an apprentice, but it's better than being a peasant.

Last week I began my apprenticeship with Master Cuthbert Ellison, an important member of the Guild of Merchant Adventurers. I am sharing a room in his household with two other boys. My duties are many, especially checking the shipments in and out of our busy warehouse. There are many rules which I must obey:

❖ Apprentices must show obedience to their betters – our Masters no less.

❖ Apprentices are not permitted to play of dice, cards or mumming.

❖ Apprentices are not permitted to drink or dance or play glitterns by night.

❖ Apprentices are not permitted to grow a beard or carry a dagger.

❖ Apprentices must not wear padded jerkins or jagged hose, even on Holy days.

I have six years to go before I become a journeyman, a trained merchant and perhaps run my own business. I have no doubt they shall be six tedious years. But at least I shall have regular food and a roof over my head. And at the end, I will have a skill to earn a good wage.

Trinity House, a mariners' guild, charged English ships two pence and foreign ships four pence for trading on the Tyne.

TUDOR 1485-1603	 STUART 1603-1714	 GEORGIAN 1714-1837	VICTORIAN 1837-1901	 MODERN TIMES 1902-NOW

Henry VIII granted charters to the Trinity House Seamen's Guild which allowed them to control shipping on the River Tyne. In return, they kept the lighthouses on the rivermouth in working order.

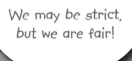

We may be strict, but we are fair!

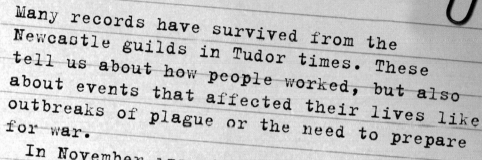

How do we know?

Many records have survived from the Newcastle guilds in Tudor times. These tell us about how people worked, but also about events that affected their lives like outbreaks of plague or the need to prepare for war.

In November 1554 the Merchant Adventurers became alarmed that their apprentices were running wild. They wrote down their concerns and these new tighter rules in their Charter and Act Book. Read this extract and use the glossary to figure out what apprentices were not allowed to do.

If speedy remedy is not found for these extravagances, this Guild cannot expect apprentices to be honest and virtuous masters themselves in the future. Consequently it is ordered...by this Merchants Court...that no Master having an apprentice will permit him to dance, dice, card or mum, or use any glitterns, or allow him to wear any cut hose...

GLOSSARY

remedy = fix
extravagance = wild behaviour
virtuous = good
permit = allow
dice = play dice games
card = play card games
mum = to act or mime
glitterns = lutes (like guitars)
cut hose = tight stockings

Civil War

The Scottish General demanded the immediate surrender of Newcastle – or he would open fire on the tower of St Nicholas Church. The Mayor, John Marley, sent a sharp reply: Fire if you wish but 'you will bathe your hands in the blood of your countrymen'. Marley had locked Scottish prisoners in the tower and dared the General to turn his cannon on it now.

During the siege, the Scottish army threatened to bombard the lantern tower of St Nicholas Church. But cunning Royalists put Scottish prisoners in the tower.

The Siege of Newcastle

Trouble began when King Charles I tried to force a Church of England prayer book on the Protestant Scots. In 1640 the Scots invaded, defeating the king. They occupied Newcastle for over a year until the king paid a huge ransom of £60,000 for them to leave.

But it got worse. In 1642, Charles quarrelled with his own Parliament and civil war broke out. In 1644 the Scottish army was back, this time supporting the Parliamentary army against the king and his Royalist army. Newcastle supported the king and became a Royalist stronghold. The Scots surrounded Newcastle. The Mayor, John Marley, refused to surrender and a nine week siege began. Finally out of patience, on 19th October 1644, cannons bombarded the city and mines blew huge gaps in the walls. At 5pm the Scots stormed the walls and took the city again. The following year, Charles I was held prisoner for a year before being sent to London for trial and eventually executed for treason in 1649.

TUDOR
1485-1603

STUART
1603-1714

GEORGIAN
1714-1837

VICTORIAN
1837-1901

MODERN
TIMES
1902-NOW

Witch Trials

After the Civil War, England was hit by witch hunts. In 1649, Newcastle employed the famous witch-hunter, Cuthbert Nicholson. Thirty women were accused of being witches and were brought to the Town Hall for questioning. Nicholson pushed a pin into their skin – if they did not bleed he declared them to be witches. Twenty-seven were found guilty and fourteen executed on the Town Moor.

Well you have a black cat – that's a sure sign you must be a witch!

Better Times

The war had stopped trade. As a result, many people went hungry during the Scottish siege and coal shipments fell. But with peace came better times and by the 1680s coal shipments had soared.

The coal trade led to a boom in shipbuilding, while this source of cheap fuel made the Tyne a centre for glassmaking, iron works and making salt from seawater. Wealth from these industries led to new building in the city. Admiring visitors declared Newcastle to be more like London than any other city in England.

Nicholson was hanged for trickery after sending 220 women to their deaths.

SPOT THIS!

Saint Nicholas Church became a cathedral in 1882. Can you spot this window?

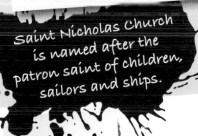
Saint Nicholas Church is named after the patron saint of children, sailors and ships.

The Guildhall and Exchange were rebuilt and fine merchants houses sprang up on the Quayside, Sandhill and the Close.

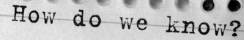
How do we know?

Newcastle was given a coat of arms and motto after the siege: 'Fortiter Defendit Triumphans' (Triumphing by a brave defence). The coat of arms and motto are carved in the seats of St Nicholas Cathedral.

The Great Flood

After three days of rain the River Tyne turned into a roaring torrent. The flood hit Newcastle early on the morning of Sunday 17th November 1771. The quayside was awash, ships were ripped from their moorings and scattered like drift wood. The medieval bridge collapsed and the shops and houses built along it plunged into the Tyne. Six people were killed and it took almost ten years to build a new bridge.

Food riots in the 1700s became known as the 'rebellions of the belly'!

Keelmen worked on keelboats carrying coal. A captain, two keel bullies and an apprentice called the Pee-Dee made up the crew.

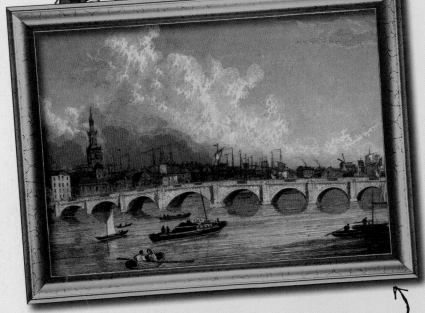

A temporary wooden bridge built after the flood was replaced with a stone bridge, built 1774-1781, which was just high enough for a keelboat to sail under.

City of Contrasts

Just as the Great Flood swept way the medieval bridge, new developments led to the demolition of the old city gates and walls. Westgate became a street of rich merchants' houses, standing in orchards and gardens, while grand areas like Charlotte Square, Hanover Square and Clavering Place were built. But alongside the wealthy lived many poor people. Neighbourhoods like Sandgate, where the keelmen and their families lived, were overcrowded and disease-ridden. Many people were often close to starvation and in 1740 and 1750 there were riots because of the high cost of food.

Coal Revolution

Industry was booming, with coal more important than ever. New, deeper pits were opened using the newest technology – steam engines – to stop them flooding. In 1765, miners at the Walker colliery dug seams of coal 182 m deep.

A network of waggonways was built to move coal from these new pits to the River Tyne. Keelmen loaded the coal into flat-bottomed keelboats. These ferried the coal to large coal ships, called colliers, waiting at the rivermouth.

By the 1770s there were around 5,000 miners in Durham and Northumberland and about 2,000 keelmen on the Tyne.

This picture of a waggonway shows a boy sitting at the back of a loaded coal wagon leading a horse.

The world-famous glass decorator, William Beilby, had his workshop at Amen Corner in the early 1760s.

Fame and Fortune

As the city grew richer Newcastle became a centre of entertainment and learning. The elegant Assembly Rooms were built in 1776 to stage grand balls, and the first Theatre Royal opened 12 years later. The Literary and Philosophical Society had one of the best libraries in the country. Great talents flourished too. Charles Avison held his first public concerts in Newcastle in 1736 and became a famous composer, while Thomas Bewick, the wood engraver, illustrated his beautiful pictures in 'A History of British Birds'.

How do we know?

Daniel Defoe, who wrote 'Robinson Crusoe', commented on the 'prodigious number' of poor in Newcastle when he visited in 1722. He also noted the magnificent Keelman's Hospital, a home for sick and retired keelmen on City Road, opened in 1701 and paid for by the keelmen.

SPOT THIS!
Can you spot the Old Assembly Rooms on Fenkle Street? Clue: today there is a conference and banqueting centre.

Railways and Bridges

On Saturday 28th September 1849, Queen Victoria and Prince Albert arrived in Newcastle to open the awesome High Level Bridge. The royal train stopped in the middle of the bridge amidst a 21-gun salute. The couple admired the spectacular view. Robert Stephenson's two-deck rail and road bridge over the Tyne was 445 metres long with the rail deck 37 metres above the river at high tide. In an age of invention, it was another example of Geordie ingenuity.

I say, could someone design a switch so that we can turn on the electric light?

For 22 years the Mauretania held the Blue Riband, the speed record for the fastest crossing of the Atlantic.

From Steam to Electricity

George and Robert Stephenson built the famous steam engine, the *Rocket,* at their Forth Road factory in 1829. When it won the Rainhill trials, Newcastle became the centre of a new industry – the railways.

In 1847, William Armstrong set up a factory at Elswick making cranes and pumps. Soon it was making guns and warships. By 1900, Armstrong was the largest employer in the North East. He was behind an amazing new Swing Bridge that swung open to allow ships upriver to his factories.

A new form of power was pioneered in Newcastle – electricity. Joseph Swan invented the incandescent lamp in 1879 and the first electric lamp factory was opened in Benwell two years later. In 1884, John Holmes designed a snap-off light switch similar to those we still use today.

Towards the end of the 1800s, Charles Parsons invented the steam turbine for generating electricity. He set up his famous Heaton Works in 1889 making turbines. One of the first ships to use the turbine was the huge liner *Mauretania*, built in Wallsend in 1907.

Rebuilding the City

Between 1825 and 1840 three men, John Dobson, an architect, Richard Grainger, a builder, and John Clayton, the town clerk, built one of the finest town centres in England. You can still walk through their elegant streets today at Eldon Square, Grainger Street and Grey Street. Dobson's greatest building, Central Station, opened in 1850. Next time you catch a train, look carefully at the curved engine shed roof. It was the first large glass and iron vaulted roof in England.

Grainger built terraced houses for Lord Armstrong's factory workers.

Grainger Street and the Grainger Market are named after their builder.

Queen Victoria's visit was reported in the London Illustrated News alongside this engraving of her arrival at Central Station.

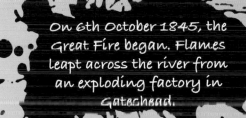

On 6th October 1845, the Great Fire began. Flames leapt across the river from an exploding factory in Gateshead.

Health and Education

Victorian Newcastle faced terrible problems with a poor water supply, slum housing and regular outbreaks of deadly diseases like cholera. Improvements came slowly after 1850. The Newcastle and Gateshead Water Company built new reservoirs in the wilds of Northumberland, piping in over 20 million gallons a day by 1914. The first public park, Leazes Park, was opened in 1873, and by the 1880s the city had more public spaces than any other town in the country. A state-of-the-art hospital, the Royal Victoria Infirmary, was opened in 1906.

SPOT THIS!

You'll have to look up to find this statue of Earl Grey in Grey Street. It's on top of a 40-metre-high column. Earl Grey didn't just make Earl Grey tea popular. He was also the British Prime Minister from 1830–34.

Billy Hepple is 11 years old. He goes to the Ragged School in Sandgate – when he isn't working as a 'shoeblack' polishing boots on the Quayside to earn his living. Billy has learned to write simple sentences and is keeping a diary. Today, 10th February 1848, he has a sad event to record.

This imaginary diary is based on the early reports of the Newcastle Ragged School. What does it tell you about the lives of street children?

Gan on, gis a hand wi' me spellin?

I haven't been to school for over a month. I'm afraid of the fever and stayed away. Just as well I did. Eddie told me that Mr Murray caught it and died. I liked old 'Mad Murray' – that's what we called him. He used to tell us off - get mad - but he was kind too.

Mr Murray saw me blacking on the Quayside and persuaded me to go to the Raggy School. 'You will get a pennyworth of bread and cheese every day, my boy,' he said. Over 40 of us street lads go to school most days. He wanted us to learn our letters and not be robbers and end up in jail.

The Raggy School is in Sandgate, one of the poorest parts of the city. Not as bad as Pandon mind. The fever liked Sandgate. Loads of the lads got it - turning blue and plopping themselves to the bones. Some went and died. But did that stop Mad Murray? Not on your life. He walked the alleys to check on 'his boys'. And it cost him. Who'll look after his wife and baby now?